Making Yo-Yos

In the quilting and sewing world, yo-yos are not the disks that travel up and down on a string, but are instead gathered fabric circles. Yo-yos have been used in quilts, garments, toys and other small items since the 1920s.

There are two types of yo-yos—finished-edge and raw-edge. Finished-edge yo-yos are used when the center of the yo-yo will be visible. Raw-edge yo-yos are used when the center of the yo-yo will be covered.

To figure out the size to cut your fabric circle for a raw-edge yo-yo, double the size of the desired finished size. That means that if you need a 2" finished raw-edge yo-yo, you should begin with a 4"-diameter circle.

To figure out the size to cut a fabric circle for a finished-edge yo-yo, double the size of the desired finished size and add ½". That means that if you need a 2" finished-edge yo-yo, you should begin with a 4½"-diameter circle.

One important thing to remember about making yo-yos is that the larger the stitch, the smaller the resulting hole in the center. So, if you want a tight hole, make larger stitches. You should experiment before beginning to stitch the yo-yos you will use in a project.

Making fabric yo-yos is easy. It is a great way to use up a lot of scraps. These little gathered fabric circles are portable and can be stitched while you wait for an appointment or for a child at a practice. They don't take long to stitch, but many projects require a large number of them, so a yo-yo project can be time consuming.

You may purchase yo-yo makers in a variety of sizes and shapes. These may be used to speed up the process because the tool folds the fabric edge under for you and provides the holes for stitching.

You may also use purchased circle templates for patterns. Any circular object that is the size of your required circle may be used for tracing shapes onto fabric. The instructions given in this book tell you to cut a specific diameter-size circle. This may be accomplished by making a template using a compass to draw the required size. You may also use patterns provided here. There is a pattern for most sizes of circles required for the projects in this book.

To join yo-yos, you can use four or six connection points as shown in Figure 1, depending on the size of the yo-yo and the purpose of the project. Using six connection points results in a sturdier connection.

This book has a variety of projects that all use fabric yo-yos in creative ways. Refer to the instructions below to help you make fast work of making a yo-yo.

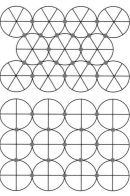

Figure 1

Steps for Making a Finished-Edge Fabric Yo-Yo

1. Thread a needle and knot the end.

2. Working with the wrong side of the fabric toward you, turn under approximately ¼" of the edge of the circle.

3. Insert the needle in the edge of the fabric on the wrong side so the knot will be inside the yo-yo as shown in Figure 2.

Figure 2

4. Sew a basic running stitch around the edge of the circle, turning the edge under as you sew as shown in Figure 3. Stop when you reach where you started.

Figure 3

House of White Birches, Berne, Indiana 46711   Clotilde.com

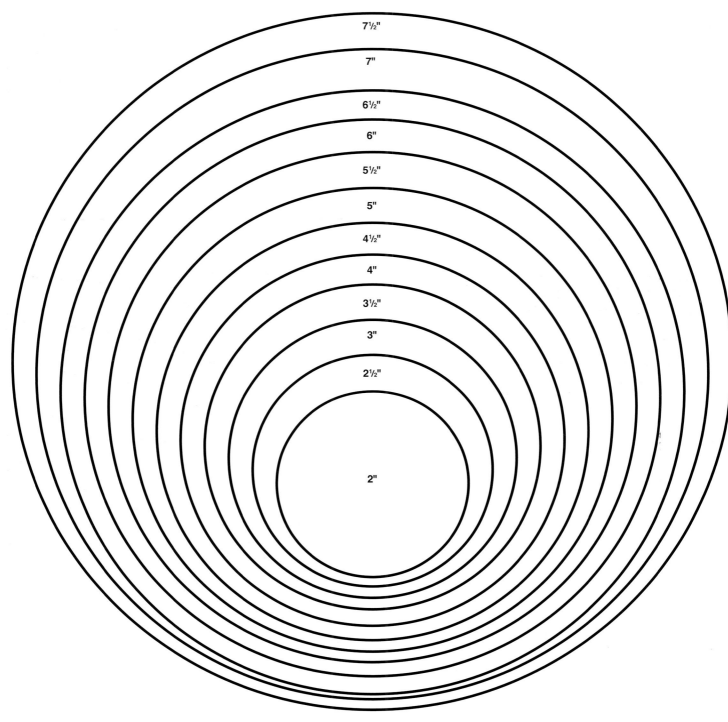

7½"
7"
6½"
6"
5½"
5"
4½"
4"
3½"
3"
2½"
2"

Yo-Yo Circles

5. Hold the needle and pull the thread to gather the circle as shown in Figure 4.

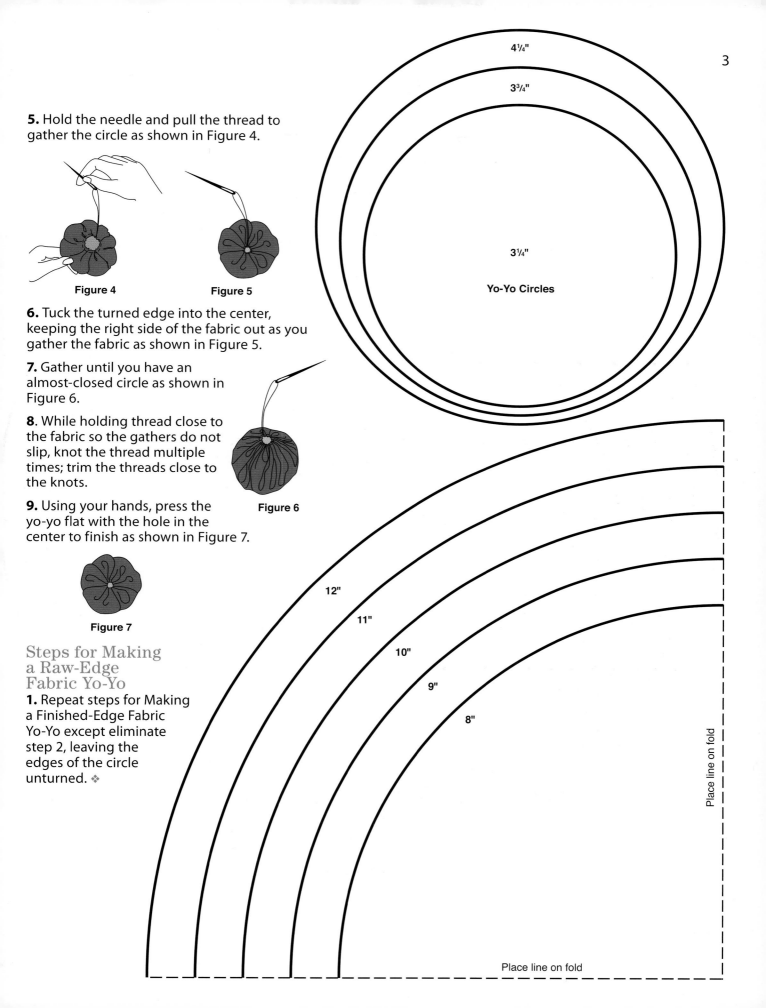

Figure 4

Figure 5

6. Tuck the turned edge into the center, keeping the right side of the fabric out as you gather the fabric as shown in Figure 5.

7. Gather until you have an almost-closed circle as shown in Figure 6.

8. While holding thread close to the fabric so the gathers do not slip, knot the thread multiple times; trim the threads close to the knots.

Figure 6

9. Using your hands, press the yo-yo flat with the hole in the center to finish as shown in Figure 7.

Figure 7

Steps for Making a Raw-Edge Fabric Yo-Yo

1. Repeat steps for Making a Finished-Edge Fabric Yo-Yo except eliminate step 2, leaving the edges of the circle unturned. ❖

4¼"

3¾"

3¼"

Yo-Yo Circles

12"

11"

10"

9"

8"

Place line on fold

Place line on fold

3

Yo-Yo Pumpkin Man

Design by Carol R. Zentgraf

Stuffed yo-yos makes this folk-art pumpkin man a little plump.

Project Specifications
Skill Level: Beginner
Doll Size: Approximately 14" tall

Materials
- 1 yard total assorted Halloween-color prints
- Scraps green, yellow and black wool felt
- ¼ yard orange wool felt
- Polyester fiberfill
- 1¼ yards ½"-wide elastic
- Black 6-strand embroidery floss
- 12-weight cotton thread
- Tapestry needle
- Scrap fusible web
- Permanent fabric adhesive
- Tracing paper
- Brown powder eye shadow and brush
- Basic sewing tools and supplies

Cutting
1. Prepare templates using patterns given; cut as directed on each piece.

2. From assorted Halloween-color prints, cut eight 7½"-diameter circles for body, (10) 6"-diameter circles for legs and (10) 5½"-diameter circles for the arms.

3. Trace the facial-feature patterns given onto the paper backing of the fusible web; cut out shapes, leaving a margin around each one. Fuse the mouth and middle-eye pieces to yellow felt, and the nose, outer-eye and center-eye pieces to the black felt. Cut pieces on traced lines; remove paper backing.

4. Prepare templates for foot, hand, head and stem pieces using patterns given; cut as directed on each piece.

Making the Yo-Yos
1. Cut a ½" slit in the center of each fabric circle. *Note: The elastic to hold the yo-yos together will fit through this opening.*

2. To make one yo-yo of any size, sew a machine gathering stitch ¼" from the edge of a fabric circle using 12-weight cotton thread in the needle and bobbin.

3. Place a small amount of fiberfill on the circle and pull the bobbin thread to gather the edges to the center until a ½"-diameter opening remains; knot thread ends to secure.

4. Repeat steps 2 and 3 to prepare all yo-yos.

Completing the Doll
1. To complete the head, join three head panels together for head front, leaving the bottom edges open; repeat with two head panels for the head back.

2. Referring to the project photo, layer and fuse the eye pieces first, and then the nose and mouth pieces to the center panel of head front.

3. Using 2 strands of embroidery floss, hand-stitch the details on the facial features referring to the project photo and mouth pattern.

4. With right sides together and the seam of the head back aligned with the center of the head front, sew the front to the back, leaving bottom edges open. Trim seam allowances where they meet at the top; turn right side out and stuff firmly with fiberfill.

5. Cut two 12" lengths of elastic for the body/legs and one 15" length for the arms. Stack the 12" lengths with ends even and zigzag-stitch together for 1" at the end as shown in Figure 1.

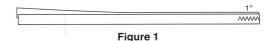

1"

Figure 1

6. Apply fabric adhesive to the stitched ends and insert inside the head; hand-sew a gathering stitch around the bottom opening of the head and pull the opening closed around the elastic. Hand-sew back and forth to secure the edges of the opening, catching the elastic in the stitching.

7. With the opening side down, slide the eight body yo-yos onto the joined elastic pieces through the openings in the yo-yos, pushing them together

until the body is 6" long; tack the opening of the bottom yo-yo around the elastic, catching the elastic in the stitching.

8. Separate the remainder of the two pieces of elastic and slide five leg yo-yos onto each piece with the gathered sides up toward the body; push them together until each leg is 5½" long. Tack the opening of the bottom yo-yo closed around the elastic, catching the elastic in the stitching.

9. To make the arms, separate the body yo-yos between the second and third yo-yos; insert the 15" length of elastic between the two body-elastic strips. Pull the elastic until it is centered on the body; slide five yo-yos onto each end of the elastic with the gathered side facing the body.

10. Push the yo-yos together to make each arm 5"

long; tack the opening of the outermost yo-yo closed around the elastic, catching the elastic in the stitching.

11. Select hand and foot pieces; pair two pieces and edgestitch together, leaving the straight edges open.

12. Edgestitch the top and side edges of the stem pieces together to ½" from the bottom as shown in Figure 2.

13. Stuff each hand and foot with fiberfill to ½" from the bottom; apply fabric adhesive to the extended elastic on each arm and leg, and insert the elastic into a hand or foot. Hand-sew a gathering stitch around the straight edge of each hand and foot piece; pull closed and stitch to secure, catching the elastic in the stitching.

½"

Figure 2

House of White Birches, Berne, Indiana 46711 Clotilde.com

14. To finish the head, use a makeup brush to apply brown powder eye shadow to the seam lines.

15. Sew the stem to the top of the head, opening the unstitched bottom to allow the piece to fit the curved area of the head as shown in Figure 3 to finish. ❖

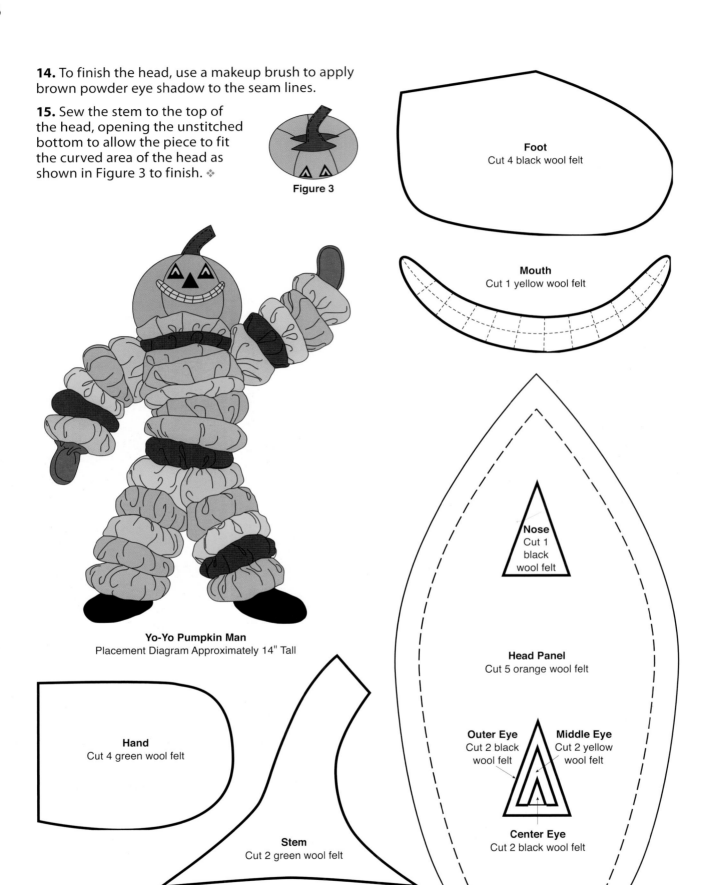

Figure 3

Foot
Cut 4 black wool felt

Mouth
Cut 1 yellow wool felt

Yo-Yo Pumpkin Man
Placement Diagram Approximately 14" Tall

Hand
Cut 4 green wool felt

Stem
Cut 2 green wool felt

Head Panel
Cut 5 orange wool felt

Nose
Cut 1 black wool felt

Outer Eye
Cut 2 black wool felt

Middle Eye
Cut 2 yellow wool felt

Center Eye
Cut 2 black wool felt

Yo-Yo Cat

Design by Carol Zentgraf

A black cat is the perfect companion for the Yo-Yo Pumpkin Man.

Project Specifications
Skill Level: Beginner
Doll Size: Approximately 14" tall

Materials
- 1 yard total assorted black prints and tonals
- Scraps green, gold, beige and red wool felt
- ¼ yard black wool felt
- Polyester fiberfill
- 1¼ yards ½"-wide elastic
- Black and red 6-strand embroidery floss
- 12-weight cotton thread
- Tapestry needle
- Scrap fusible web
- Permanent fabric adhesive
- Tracing paper
- Basic sewing tools and supplies

Cutting
1. Prepare templates using patterns given on pages 8 and 9.

2. From assorted black prints and tonals, cut eight 7½"-diameter circles for body, (10) 6"-diameter circles for legs and (10) 5½"-diameter circles for the arms.

3. Trace the facial-feature and inner-ear patterns given onto the paper backing of the fusible web; cut out shapes, leaving a margin around each one. Fuse the nose to red felt, iris pieces to green felt, eye pieces to gold felt and inner-ear pieces to beige felt. Cut pieces on traced lines; remove paper backing.

4. Cut foot, hand, head and ear pieces as directed on patterns.

Making the Yo-Yos
1. Cut a ½" slit in the center of each fabric circle. *Note: The elastic to hold the yo-yos together will fit through this opening.*

2. To make one yo-yo of any size, sew a machine gathering stitch ¼" from the edge of a fabric circle using 12-weight cotton thread in the needle and bobbin.

3. Place a small amount of fiberfill on the circle and pull the bobbin thread to gather the edges to the center until a ½"-diameter opening remains; knot thread ends to secure.

4. Repeat steps 2 and 3 to prepare all yo-yos.

Completing the Doll

1. Fuse the inner ear pieces to two ear pieces.

2. Stack one plain ear and one fused ear; edgestitch together. Repeat for the second ear.

3. To complete the head, join three head panels together for head front, leaving the bottom edges open; repeat with two head panels for the head back.

4. Position an ear right sides together 1" from the center seam on each side edge of the head front panel as shown in Figure 1; baste the ears to the head.

Figure 1

5. With right sides together and the seam of the head back aligned with the center of the head front, sew the front to the back, leaving bottom edges open. Trim seam allowance where they meet at the top; turn right side out.

6. Referring to the project photo, layer and fuse the eye pieces first, and then the iris and nose pieces to the head front referring to Figure 2 for positioning.

Figure 2

7. Using 3 strands of red embroidery floss, hand-stitch the mouth shape using pattern given as a guide, again referring to Figure 2.

8. Stuff head firmly with fiberfill.

9. Cut two 12" lengths of elastic for the body/legs and one 15" length for the arms. Stack the 12" lengths with ends even and zigzag-stitch together for 1" at the end as shown in Figure 3.

Figure 3

10. Apply fabric adhesive to the stitched ends and insert inside the head; hand-sew a gathering stitch around the bottom opening of the head and pull the opening closed around the elastic. Hand-sew back and forth to secure the edges of the opening, catching the elastic in the stitching.

11. With the opening side down, slide the eight body yo-yos onto the joined elastic pieces through the openings in the yo-yos, pushing them together until the body is 6" long; tack the opening of the bottom yo-yo around the elastic, catching the elastic in the stitching.

12. Separate the remainder of the two pieces of elastic and slide five leg yo-yos onto each piece with the gathered sides up toward the body; push them together until each leg is 5½" long. Tack the opening of the bottom yo-yo closed around the elastic, catching the elastic in the stitching.

13. To make the arms, separate the body yo-yos between the second and third yo-yos; insert the 15" length of elastic between the two body-elastic strips. Pull the elastic until it is centered on the body; slide five yo-yos onto each end of the elastic with the gathered side facing the body.

14. Push the yo-yos together to make each arm 5" long; tack the opening of the outermost yo-yo closed around the elastic, catching the elastic in the stitching.

15. Select hand and foot pieces; pair two pieces and edgestitch together, leaving the straight edges open.

16. Stuff each hand with fiberfill to ½" from the opening; apply fabric adhesive to the extended elastic on each arm and insert the elastic in a hand. Hand-sew a gathering stitch around each hand at the bottom of the stitching; pull closed and stitch to secure, catching the elastic in the stitching.

17. Repeat step 16 with feet at bottom of legs to finish. ❖

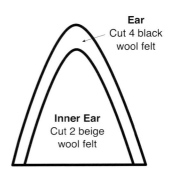

Ear
Cut 4 black
wool felt

Inner Ear
Cut 2 beige
wool felt

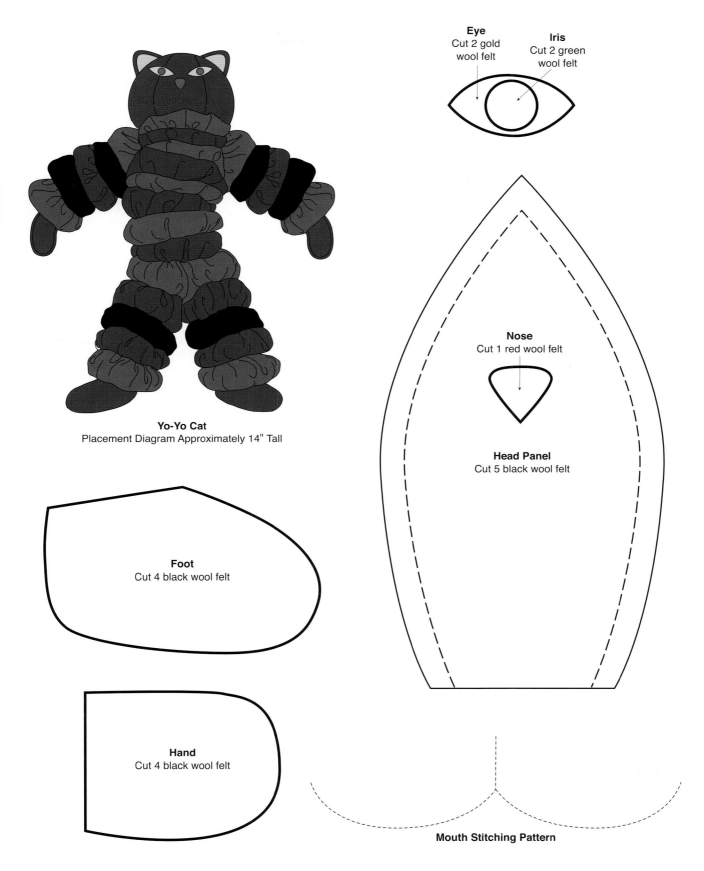

Eye
Cut 2 gold
wool felt

Iris
Cut 2 green
wool felt

Yo-Yo Cat
Placement Diagram Approximately 14" Tall

Nose
Cut 1 red wool felt

Head Panel
Cut 5 black wool felt

Foot
Cut 4 black wool felt

Hand
Cut 4 black wool felt

Mouth Stitching Pattern

Jeepers Creepers Halloween Wreaths

Designs by Helen Rafson

Decorate either a small or large space with a simple-to-make spooky yo-yo wreath.

Large Wreath

Project Specifications
Skill Level: Beginner
Wreath Size: 12" diameter

Materials
- 5 (2" x 18") strips orange print
- 7 (8" x 16") pieces coordinating orange prints
- Orange all-purpose thread
- Craft glue
- Thick designer glue
- 12"-diameter molded foam wreath
- Buttons: 1 each 7/8" jack-o'-lantern and 1" spider on web; 2 each 7/8" orange hearts, 15/16" black spiders and 15/16" black cat; and 4 (5/8") yellow stars
- 1 7/8" yellow satin puffy star
- 48" (1½"-wide) black satin ribbon
- Tab hanger
- Basic sewing tools and supplies

Cutting
1. Cut two 5½"-diameter circles from each of the seven 8" x 16" strips coordinating orange prints.

Making the Yo-Yos
1. Make 14 finished-edge yo-yos referring to Making Yo-Yos on page 1.

Completing the Large Wreath
1. Use craft glue to glue one end of one 2" x 18" strip of orange print fabric to bottom of foam wreath; wrap strip around wreath, overlapping slightly and gluing opposite end. Repeat with remaining 2" x 18" strips, cutting away excess fabric if necessary.

2. Flatten yo-yos with gathers at center top. Using photo as a guide, glue yo-yos around wreath using craft glue, overlapping slightly; let dry.

3. Tie ribbon in bow with long streamers; glue to the center bottom of the wreath using craft glue.

4. Glue buttons to wreath using thick designer glue, referring to project photo for positioning suggestions.

5. Using thick designer glue for remainder of gluing, glue yellow satin puffy star behind one orange heart, and yellow stars over and around opposite orange heart. Glue tab hanger to center top of wreath on back to finish.

Small Wreath

Project Specifications
Skill Level: Beginner
Wreath Size: 5" diameter

Materials
- 4 (1" x 16") strips orange print
- 6 (4" x 8") pieces coordinating orange prints
- Scraps batting
- Orange all-purpose thread
- Craft glue
- 6" x 11" piece poster board
- Thick designer glue
- Buttons: 2 each 1" spider on web and 7/8" jack-o'-lanterns; and 3 (½") ghosts
- 7/16" black button
- 16" each black, gold and orange ⅛"-wide satin ribbon
- Tab hanger
- Basic sewing tools and supplies

Cutting
1. Cut two 3"-diameter circles from each of the six 4" x 8" strips of coordinating orange prints.

2. Prepare template using small wreath pattern given; cut two wreaths from poster board and three wreaths from batting.

Making the Yo-Yos
1. Make 12 finished-edge yo-yos referring to Making Yo-Yos on page 1.

Completing the Small Wreath

1. Glue layers of batting between poster board wreaths using craft glue; let dry.

2. Glue 1" x 16" strips of orange print fabric around poster board wreath form as instructed in step 1 of Completing the Large Wreath.

3. Repeat step 2 of Completing the Large Wreath.

4. Holding ⅛"-wide ribbons together, tie in a bow.

5. Using craft glue, glue bow to center bottom of wreath and black button over bow knot.

6. Referring to photo, use thick designer glue to adhere craft buttons on wreath. Glue tab hanger to center top of wreath on back to finish. ❖

Jeepers Creepers Small Halloween Wreath
Placement Diagram 5" diameter

Jeepers Creepers Halloween Wreath
Placement Diagram 12" diameter

Small Wreath Pattern
Cut 2 poster board & 3 batting

House of White Birches, Berne, Indiana 46711   Clotilde.com

Yo-Yo Pumpkin Pin

Design by Chris Malone

Get in the spirit of Halloween by wearing a simple-to-make yo-yo pumpkin pin.

Project Specifications
Skill Level: Beginner
Pin Size: 3" x 3½"

Materials
- 8" x 8" square orange tonal or print
- 2½" length of ⅜"-wide green or brown grosgrain ribbon
- 10" length of plastic-coated, 18-gauge, green or bronze craft wire
- All-purpose thread to match fabric
- Fray preventative
- Permanent fabric adhesive
- Pencil
- 1" pin back
- Basic sewing tools and supplies

Cutting
1. Cut a 7½"-diameter circle orange tonal or print.

Completing the Pin

1. Make a finished-edge yo-yo from the orange circle referring to Making Yo-Yos on page 1, pulling the hole toward the top instead of center as shown in Figure 1.

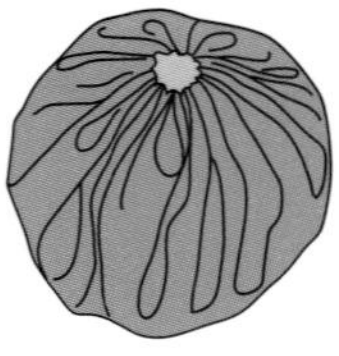

Figure 1

2. Bend the wire in half and curl each side by wrapping it around the pencil, changing directions as shown in Figure 2.

Figure 2

Figure 3

3. Tie a single knot about ½" from one end of the ribbon. Trim the other end at an angle as shown in Figure 3; apply fray preventative to the angled end.

4. Poke the short end of the ribbon into the hole at the top of the yo-yo so the knot fills the hole; push the bent center of the wire behind the ribbon knot.

Apply a few dots of fabric adhesive to hold the ribbon and wire in place.

5. Sew the pin back near the top of the back side of the yo-yo to complete the pin. ❖

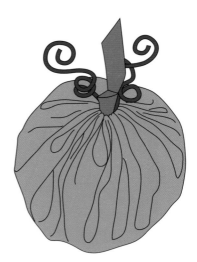

Yo-Yo Pumpkin Pin
Placement Diagram 3" x 3½"

Yo-Yo Wreath

Design by Carol Zentgraf

Decorate your door with this fun wreath.

Project Specifications
Skill Level: Beginner
Wreath Size: Approximately 12" diameter

Materials
- ½ yard green print to wrap wreath
- 1½ yards total assorted green and red prints for yo-yos
- 12"-diameter plastic foam wreath form
- All-purpose thread to match fabrics
- Extra-large yo-yo maker (optional)
- Permanent fabric adhesive
- Basic sewing tools and supplies

Cutting
1. Cut seven 2" by fabric width strips green print to wrap wreath.

Yo-Yo Wreath
Placement Diagram Approximately 12" diameter

Making the Yo-Yos
1. Prepare 58 yo-yos using green and red prints, and the extra-large yo-yo maker, referring to the manufacturer's instructions.

2. To prepare yo-yos without the yo-yo maker, cut (58) 5½"-diameter circles from red and green prints; complete finished-edge yo-yos referring to Making Yo-Yos on page 1.

Completing the Wreath
1. Glue one end of one 2" strip to the back of the plastic foam wreath. Wrap strip around wreath and glue opposite end to the back. Repeat with remaining strips to cover surface of wreath.

2. Arrange 24 yo-yos in a single layer on outside edge of wreath, overlapping edges. Carefully lift each yo-yo and glue in place.

3. Repeat step 2 to glue 14 yo-yos around inside edge of wreath and 20 yo-yos over the front of the wreath. Let glue dry. ❖

Santa Loves Yo-Yos

Design by Julie Higgins

Even Santa can't resist the little gathered fabric circles called yo-yos.

Project Specifications
Skill Level: Intermediate
Santa Size: Approximately 10" tall seated

Materials
- Scrap dark peach solid
- ⅛ yard muslin
- ⅛ yard black tonal
- ½ yard burgundy solid
- All-purpose thread to match fabrics
- Large yo-yo maker (optional)
- 1 small, 2 medium and 2 medium/large gold jingle bells
- Polyester fiberfill
- Heavy-duty or carpet thread
- Black or brown permanent fabric pen
- Rose fabric marker or crayon
- 1" x 36" piece faux fur
- 2" (⅜"-wide) black ribbon
- Fiber for beard, mustache and hair (raw wool used in sample)
- Permanent fabric adhesive
- Marking pencil or air-soluble marking pen
- 1 pair gold doll glasses
- Card stock
- Basic sewing tools and supplies

Cutting
1. Cut four 7" x 6" pieces burgundy solid for hat and suit.

2. Cut two 2⅝" x 6" pieces dark peach solid for face/head.

3. Prepare Santa trimming template and nose template using patterns given.

Making the Yo-Yos
1. Complete seven muslin, six black tonal and 20 burgundy solid yo-yos using the large yo-yo maker referring to manufacturer's instructions, or cut 4"-diameter circles from fabrics in numbers listed and refer to Making Yo-Yos on page 1 to make finished-edge yo-yos.

Completing the Doll
1. Join two 7" x 6" burgundy solid pieces with one dark peach piece to make one Santa unit as shown in Figure 1; press seams away from the dark peach piece. Repeat to make two Santa units.

Figure 1

2. Using the full-size face pattern given on Santa trimming pattern, draw eyes and mouth on the face with black or brown permanent fabric pen.

3. Use a rose marker or crayon to color cheeks and smile.

4. Use nose pattern given to make a template from card stock; trace around template on dark peach solid. Cut out, adding ¼" seam allowance around when cutting.

5. Sew a running or basting stitch around the marked line; do not end thread. Place the card-stock template on the wrong side of the fabric and pull the basting stitches to gather nose piece around the card-stock template as shown in Figure 2; knot thread to secure gathering.

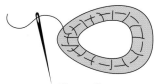

Figure 2

6. Remove card-stock template and place fiberfill in the gathered nose. *Note: If you want a smaller nose, pull gathering stitches without using the card-stock template.*

7. Pin nose to face area as marked on Santa trimming pattern; hand-stitch in place.

8. Place the Sant unit front and back pieces right sides together; place the Santa trimming pattern on the layered pieces and trim to match pattern as shown in Figure 3. Stitch all around, leaving an opening as marked on pattern.

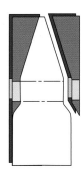

Figure 3

9. Before turning right side out, align bottom seam with side seam and stitch ¾" from point to make a square bottom as shown in Figure 4. Repeat on the other side and bottom seams. Trim seam to ¼", again referring to Figure 4.

¾" ¼"

Figure 4

10. Turn right side out through opening. Using the full-size pattern, mark a line on the bottom of the hat area as shown in Figure 5; stitch on the marked line.

11. Stuff fiberfill through opening to create a firm, full doll.

12. Turn opening edges to the inside; hand-stitch opening closed.

13. Measure around head at hat line; cut a piece of faux fur the measured length plus ¼"; trim to ½" wide. Hand-stitch the fur strip in place, overlapping at center back.

Figure 5

14. Repeat step 13 for front edges and bottom of jacket as marked on pattern for placement. Before sewing the front-edge pieces in place, place the piece of black ribbon on the jacket front for belt as marked on pattern; glue ends of ribbon in place to secure.

15. To make an arm, using an 18" piece of doubled heavy-duty thread, string five burgundy yo-yos, one muslin yo-yo and one medium jingle bell onto the thread in that order. Run the same thread back through the string of yo-yos to exit at the beginning stitch.

16. Secure thread ends and then, using the same thread, attach the yo-yo string to side of the Santa body at the top of the jacket piece.

17. Repeat steps 15 and 16 to attach the second arm.

18. Repeat steps 15 and 16 with five burgundy, two muslin and three black tonal yo-yos, and one medium/large bell, in that order for each leg, and stitch just below jacket trim to finish the body.

19. Referring to the photo and the Placement Diagram, fold hat tip down; sew one muslin yo-yo

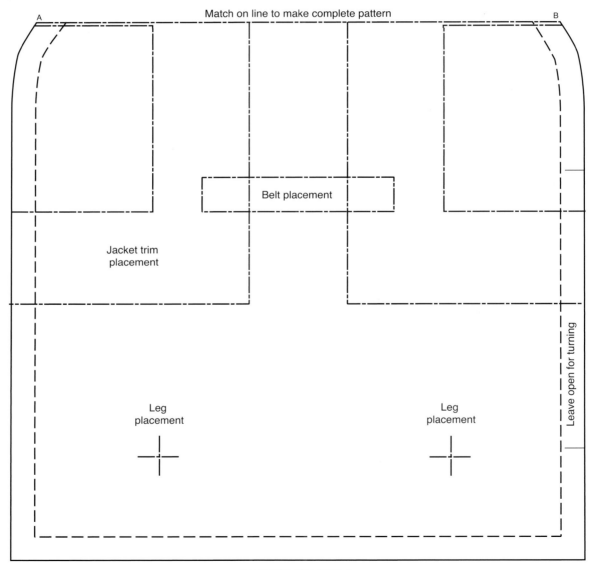

Match on line to make complete pattern

A   B

Belt placement

Jacket trim
placement

Leave open for turning

Leg
placement

Leg
placement

Santa Trimming Pattern

1½" from the tip. Sew the small bell in the center of the yo-yo.

20. Using fiber of choice, glue a little on the back of Santa's head right under the bottom of his hat. Glue a small piece under the nose for a mustache and strips around the jaw line up to his hat for whiskers.

21. Poke ends of glasses wire into Santa's head and attach with glue to finish. ❖

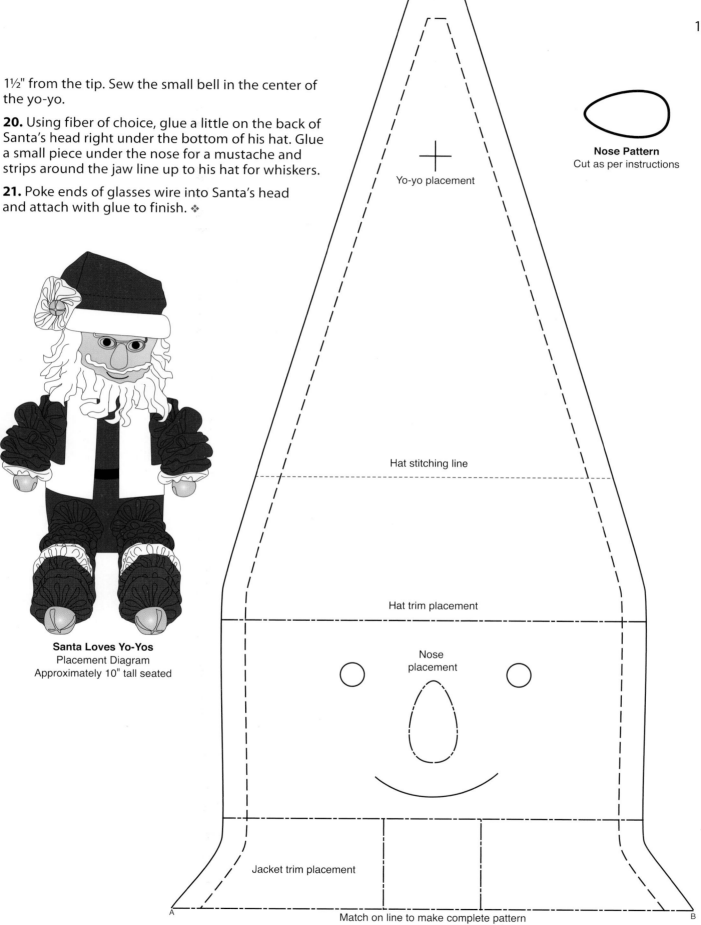

Santa Loves Yo-Yos
Placement Diagram
Approximately 10" tall seated

Nose Pattern
Cut as per instructions

Yo-yo placement

Hat stitching line

Hat trim placement

Nose placement

Jacket trim placement

A

Match on line to make complete pattern

B

House of White Birches, Berne, Indiana 46711 Clotilde.com

Smiling Elf

Design by Julie Higgins

Make several little elves to help Santa during the holidays!

Project Specifications
Skill Level: Intermediate
Elf Size: Approximately 8" tall seated

Materials for 1 Elf
- 1 fat eighth print for scarf and yo-yos
- 10" x 12" plaid for hat
- 12" x 12" dark peach solid
- 1 fat quarter print/plaid for shirt and yo-yos
- 1 fat quarter coordinating solid/tonal for pants and yo-yos
- 17 coordinating 3" x 3" squares for yo-yos
- All-purpose thread to match fabrics
- Small yo-yo maker (optional)
- 3 small and 2 medium gold jingle bells
- Polyester fiberfill
- Heavy-duty or carpet thread
- Black or brown permanent fabric pen
- Rose fabric marker or crayon
- ½ yard (⅜"-wide) gold trim or ribbon
- Permanent fabric adhesive
- Marking pencil or air-soluble marking pen
- Card stock
- Basic sewing tools and supplies

Cutting
1. Prepare templates for ear and nose using pattern pieces given.

2. Cut two 4½" x 5½" plaid A pieces for hat.

3. Cut two 4½" x 2⅛" dark peach solid B for face/head.

4. Cut two 4½" x 3" print C for shirt.

5. Cut two 4½" x 3" coordinating solid/tonal D for pants.

6. Cut one 1" x 14" print strip for scarf.

7. Prepare elf-trimming template using pattern given.

Making the Yo-Yos
1. Complete 37 yo-yos using the small yo-yo maker referring to manufacturer's instructions, or cut (37) 3"-diameter circles and refer to Making Yo-Yos on page 1 to make finished-edge yo-yos. **Note:** Six

yo-yos on the top of each leg match the pants fabric; the remaining five yo-yos on each leg are cut from coordinating fabric squares. The arms use six from coordinating fabric squares and six from the shirt fabric. The hat uses two from the scarf fabric and one from a coordinating fabric square. Refer to project photo for color suggestions and placement of yo-yos.

Completing the Doll
1. Cut two 3" and two 3½" lengths gold trim or ribbon.

2. Place the 3" lengths on one C piece 1¼" from outer edge as marked on pattern; stitch trim in place.

3. Place the 3½" lengths on the remaining C piece starting 1¼" from the bottom of one side edge diagonally to the opposite side top edge as marked on pattern with red lines; stitch trim in place.

4. Join one each A, B, C and D piece on the 4½" sides to make a body unit referring to Figure 1; press seams in one direction. Repeat to make two elf units.

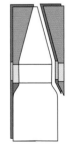

Figure 1   **Figure 2**

5. Place the elf unit right sides together; place the full-size trimming pattern on the layered pieces and trim to match pattern as shown in Figure 2. Transfer all placement and stitching markings.

6. Lay two pieces of dark peach solid fabric right sides together. Using the ear template, trace two ears on the layered fabric. Cut out two sets of ears, adding a ¼" seam allowance all around each set.

7. With right sides together, sew on the marked line, leaving the short edge open; trim seam to ⅛". Turn right side out and press.

8. Lightly stuff ears with fiberfill; topstitch through both layers and stuffing to stitch inner-ear lines as marked on pattern and as shown in Figure 3.

9. Position ear pieces on the elf front piece with the unfinished edges of ears even with outside edge of the face as marked on pattern; baste to hold in place.

Figure 3

10. Using the full-size face pattern given on elf trimming pattern, draw eyes and mouth on the face with black or brown permanent fabric pen.

11. Using a rose marker or crayon, color cheeks, smile and the tips of his ears.

12. Use nose pattern given to make a template from card stock; trace around template on dark peach sold. Cut out, adding ¼" seam allowance around when cutting.

13. Sew a running or basting stitch around the marked line; do not end thread. Place the card-stock template on the wrong side of the fabric and pull the basting stitches to gather nose piece around the template as shown in Figure 4; knot thread to secure gathering.

Figure 4

14. Remove template and place fiberfill in the gathered nose. ***Note:*** *If you want a smaller nose, pull gathering stitches without using the template.*

15. Pin nose to face area as marked on body pattern; hand-stitch in place.

16. Place the elf unit front and back pieces right sides together; stitch all around, leaving an opening as marked on pattern.

17. Before turning right side out, align bottom seam with side seam and stitch ¾" from point to make a square bottom as shown in Figure 5.

¾"   ¼"

Figure 5

Repeat on the other side and bottom seams. Trim seam to ¼", again referring to Figure 5.

18. Turn right side out through opening. Using the full-size pattern, mark a line on the bottom of the hat area as shown in Figure 6; stitch on the marked line.

19. Stuff fiberfill through opening to create a firm, full doll.

20. Turn opening edges to the inside; hand-stitch opening closed.

21. Fold ears toward the back of the head and tack in place as shown in Figure 7 to resemble elf ears.

22. Using an 18" piece of doubled heavy-duty thread, string six arm yo-yos and one small jingle bell onto the thread. Run the same thread back through the string of yo-yos to exit at the beginning stitch.

Figure 6

Figure 7

23. Secure thread ends and then, using the same thread, attach the yo-yo string to side of the elf body at the top of the C shirt piece.

24. Repeat steps 21 and 22 to attach the second arm.

25. Repeat steps 21 and 22 with 11 leg yo-yos and one medium bell for each leg, stitching yo-yo legs in place at bottom edge of pants to finish the body.

26. Repeat steps 21 and 22 with three hat yo-yos and a small bell and stitch to the tip of the hat. Fold hat tip down; tack in place at stitching line if desired.

27. Tie the 1" x 14" scarf strip around the neck to complete the elf doll. ❖

Smiling Elf
Placement Diagram Approximately 8" tall seated

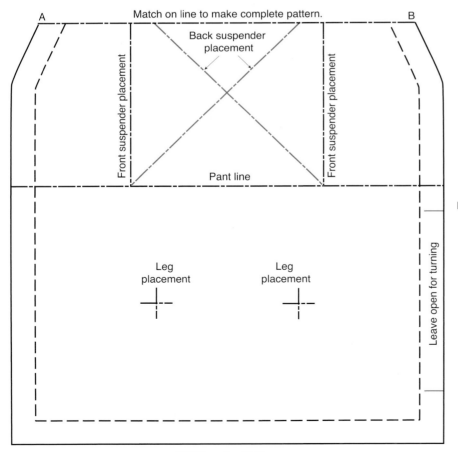

Elf Trimming Pattern

A — Match on line to make complete pattern. — B

Back suspender placement

Front suspender placement

Front suspender placement

Pant line

Leg placement

Leg placement

Leave open for turning

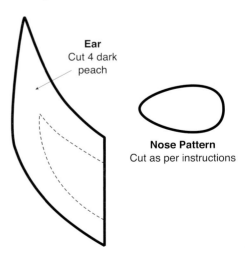

Ear
Cut 4 dark peach

Nose Pattern
Cut as per instructions

Hat stitching line

Ear placement

Nose placement

Ear placement

A

Match on line to make complete pattern.

1"

B

House of White Birches, Berne, Indiana 46711   Clotilde.com

Yo-Yo Ornaments

Designs by Carol Zentgraf

Whether you make the snowman ornament with just two yo-yos or the tree ornament with 10 yo-yos, you will have fun in the process.

Snowman Ornament

Project Specifications
Skill Level: Beginner
Snowman Size: Approximately 5" tall and 2½" wide at base

Materials
- Scraps white tonal and red print
- Black, green, red and orange felt scraps
- All-purpose thread to match fabrics
- 6" each ¼"-wide and ⅛"-wide red ribbon
- Black wool roving
- Felting needle
- Scrap of upholstery foam
- Extra-small, large and extra-large yo-yo makers (optional)
- Permanent fabric adhesive
- Basic sewing tools and supplies

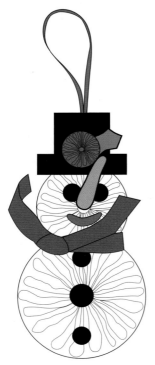

Snowman Ornament
Placement Diagram Approximately
5" tall and 2½" wide at base

Cutting
1. Prepare templates for holly leaf, hat, nose and mouth using patterns given. Cut as directed on patterns.

Making the Yo-Yos
1. Referring to manufacturer's instructions, use yo-yo maker to make one extra-small yo-yo from red print, and one each large and extra-large yo-yos from white tonal.

2. To prepare yo-yos without yo-yo maker, cut one 2"-diameter circle from red print, and one each 4"- and 5½"-diameter circles from white tonal. Refer to Making Yo-Yos on page 1 to complete a finished-edge yo-yo from each circle.

Completing the Snowman Ornament
1. Whipstitch the two white yo-yos together as shown in Figure 1 to make snowman body/head unit.

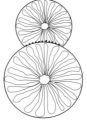

Figure 1

2. Apply a thin layer of fabric adhesive to one side of the felt nose and roll it up to form a cone; glue into the center opening of the small yo-yo head.

3. Layer and edgestitch the two hat pieces together along the side and top edges, catching the ends of the ⅛" ribbon in the stitching between the hat layers on the top of hat to form a loop for hanging as shown in Figure 2.

4. Glue the open edges of the hat bottom to front and back of the yo-yo head.

Figure 2

5. Glue the holly leaf and red yo-yo to the hat.

6. To make eyes and buttons, roll five small balls of black wool roving. Place each ball on the piece of foam and punch with the felting needle until the fibers interlock to make a solid ball.

7. Glue balls in place on the snowman body referring to the Placement Diagram for positioning.

8. Tie the ¼"-wide ribbon around the neck to complete the Snowman Ornament.

Tree Ornament

Project Specifications
Skill Level: Beginner
Tree Size: Approximately 4" x 5"

Materials
- Scraps green prints
- Scrap brown print
- Scrap gold felt
- All-purpose thread to match fabrics
- 6" (⅛"-wide) red ribbon
- Small yo-yo maker (optional)
- Permanent fabric adhesive
- Basic sewing tools and supplies

Tree Ornament
Placement Diagram 4" x 5"

Cutting
1. Prepare template for star using pattern given. Cut as directed on pattern.

Making the Yo-Yos
1. Referring to manufacturer's instructions, use yo-yo maker to make one brown and 10 green yo-yos.

2. To prepare yo-yos without yo-yo maker, cut one brown and 10 green 3"-diameter circles. Refer to Making Yo-Yos on page 1 to complete finished-edge yo-yos.

Completing the Tree Ornament

1. Arrange the green yo-yos in rows referring to the Placement Diagram; whipstitch edges together to make the tree shape.

2. Center the brown yo-yo and whipstitch edges to the tree shape.

3. Layer the two star pieces; insert ribbon ends and glue to hold.

4. Edgestitch the two star shapes together all around, catching the ends of the ribbon in the stitching on the top to form a loop for hanging.

5. Stitch star to the top of the tree shape to complete the Tree Ornament.

Candy Cane Ornament

Project Specifications
Skill Level: Beginner
Candy Cane Size: Approximately 3" x 6½"

Materials
- Scraps white tonal and red print
- All-purpose thread to match fabrics
- ⅔ yard ⅛"-wide red ribbon
- Small yo-yo maker (optional)
- Permanent fabric adhesive
- Basic sewing tools and supplies

Making the Yo-Yos

1. Referring to manufacturer's instructions, use yo-yo maker to make five white tonal and six red print yo-yos

2. To prepare yo-yos without yo-yo maker, cut five white tonal and six red print 3"-diameter circles. Refer to Making Yo-Yos on page 1 to complete finished-edge yo-yos.

Completing the Candy Cane Ornament

1. Arrange the white and red yo-yos to make a candy-cane shape, overlapping yo-yos as needed, referring to the Placement Diagram; secure in place with fabric adhesive.

2. Whipstitch edges together on the fronts and backs to make the shape.

3. Form a loop for hanging in the center of the ribbon and make a knot; wrap ends around the top of the candy cane and tie into a bow to complete the Candy Cane Ornament. ❖

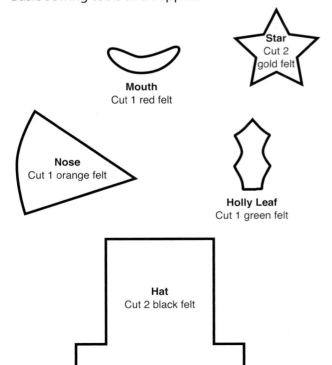

Mouth
Cut 1 red felt

Star
Cut 2
gold felt

Nose
Cut 1 orange felt

Holly Leaf
Cut 1 green felt

Hat
Cut 2 black felt

Candy Cane Ornament
Placement Diagram Approximately 3" x 6½"

Yo-Yo Christmas Tree

Design by Linda Turner Griepentrog

Add yuletide cheer to your holiday table with a simple-to-make yo-yo tree.

Project Note

The yo-yo sections can be gathered by hand or machine, and a bit of stuffing keeps them puffy. For a true sewing-inspired touch, use a wooden thread spool as the base.

Project Specifications

Skill Level: Beginner
Tree Size: 14" tall

Materials

- 10 scraps assorted green prints
- Green all-purpose thread
- 16" (¼"-diameter) wooden dowel
- 1½" x 2⅛" wooden spool
- 2 (1⅞") star buttons
- Polyester fiberfill
- Red and green pearl cotton
- Fabric glue
- Green and gold metallic acrylic paint
- Small paintbrush
- Compass or circle templates
- Basic sewing tools and supplies

Cutting

1. Using a compass or circle template, cut 10 circles in 1" increments from 12" to 3" in diameter.

Making the Yo-Yo Flowers

1. Fold and crease each circle to find the center.

2. Cut a very small slit (less than ¼") in the creased center of each circle.

3. Referring to Making Yo-Yos on page 1, baste ⅛" from raw edge of each yo-yo circle with knotted thread; pull up thread to gather and lightly stuff each circle with fiberfill before tying off thread ends.

Completing the Tree

1. Using metallic acrylic paints, paint the wooden dowel with green; paint the wooden spool with gold. Let dry.

2. Wind red pearl cotton snugly around wooden spool using a drop of fabric glue at the beginning and end to anchor.

3. Glue at least ½" of wooden dowel in the hole in the spool; let dry.

4. With gathered sides of yo-yos facing up, insert dowel through center slits of the nine yo-yos, from larger to smaller.

5. Leaving room at the top of the dowel for the star buttons, arrange yo-yos to fill the space. Secure positions with glue if necessary.

6. Slide the tenth yo-yo over the top of the dowel, gathered side down.

7. Tie green pearl cotton through holes in star buttons. Glue buttons to the top of the dowel. ❖

Yo-Yo Christmas Tree
Placement Diagram 14" tall

Yo-Yo Angel Ornament

Design by Chris Malone

Dig out your scraps and make a bunch of these little cuties for your holiday tree.

Project Specifications
Skill Level: Beginner
Ornament Size: 3" x 4¼"

Materials
- 2 (8" x 8") squares coordinating red-and-green prints (wings and dress)
- 1"-diameter two-holed ecru or pale pink button
- 6" textured doll-hair yarn
- 4" mini green garland
- Small brass heart charm
- 3" metallic gold cord
- All-purpose thread to match fabrics
- Black 6-strand embroidery floss
- 8" green pearl cotton or cord
- Large-eye embroidery needle
- Permanent fabric adhesive
- Basic sewing tools and supplies

Cutting
1. Cut one 7½"-diameter circle from one print for wings, and one 6½"-diameter circle from second print for dress.

Completing the Ornament
1. Make a finished-edge yo-yo from the dress circle referring to Making Yo-Yos on page 1, pulling the hole toward the top instead of center as shown in Figure 1.

Figure 1

Figure 2

2. Repeat with the wings yo-yo, except after gathering and knotting the thread, wrap it loosely around the center of the fabric, forming two rounded wings as shown in Figure 2.

3. Place a button at the top edge of the dress yo-yo, covering the hole, and attach by stitching through the fabric and the holes with 3 strands of black embroidery floss.

4. To make the angel's hair, wrap the hair yarn around a finger several times; slip the bundle of yarn off the finger and wrap thread around the center; knot to secure as shown in Figure 3. Glue in place on top of button, referring to the Placement Diagram and project photo for positioning.

Figure 3

Figure 4

5. Shape the mini garland into a 2" circle; overlap the ends and wrap together as shown in Figure 4. Cut off any excess.

6. Apply fabric adhesive to the overlapped section and insert between the back of the head (button) and dress.

7. Thread the charm onto the gold cord; tie a knot about ¾" above the charm. Apply fabric adhesive to the knot and insert it under the bottom or "chin" area of the button as shown in Figure 5.

Figure 5   **Figure 6**

8. Center and glue the top of the dress to the wings so the gathered side of both yo-yos are on top as shown in Figure 6.

9. Thread the green pearl cotton or cord onto a needle and take a small stitch at the top edge of the dress; tie a knot at the ends. Slide the knot down to the fabric and add a dot of fabric adhesive to secure and finish. ❖

Yo-Yo Angel Ornament
Placement Diagram 3" x 4¼"

Yo-Yo Christmas Throw

Design by Carol Zentgraf

Add a joyful spot to your holiday home with this easy throw made with giant-size yo-yos.

Project Specifications
Skill Level: Beginner
Throw Size: 40" x 50"

Materials
- 3½ yards total assorted green prints, each at least ⅓ yard
- 5¼ yards total assorted red prints, each at least ⅓ yard
- Red and green all-purpose thread
- Basic sewing tools and supplies

Cutting
1. Cut (32) 11"-diameter circles green prints.

2. Cut (48) 11"-diameter circles red prints.

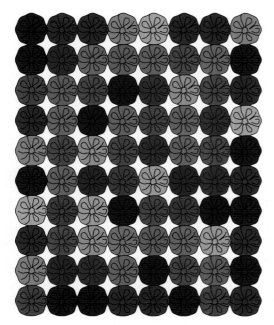

Yo-Yo Christmas Throw
Placement Diagram 40" x 50"

Making the Yo-Yos
1. Complete finished-edge yo-yos referring to Making Yo-Yos on page 1, except turn under ½" and leave a ½" opening in each yo-yo.

Completing the Throw
1. Position opening in center top of each yo-yo and finger-press edges.

2. On large flat surface, arrange red print yo-yos in six rows of eight yo-yos each.

3. Referring to Making Yo-Yos on page 1 , hand-stitch yo-yos together in rows with matching thread, making sure stitches are secure. Join the rows to complete the center of the throw.

4. Referring to the Placement Diagram, hand-stitch green yo-yos all around center to form a border. ❖

House of White Birches, Berne, Indiana 46711   Clotilde.com

Yo-Yo Ho-Ho Santa

Design by Carol Zentgraf

Yo-yos make the perfect design element to make Santa's beard in this unique holiday wall hanging.

Project Specifications
Skill Level: Beginner
Santa Size: 14" x 28"

Materials
- Fat quarter white/silver print
- Scraps black and red felt
- ¼ yard pink solid
- 1 yard red/white print
- 1⅛ yards white tonal
- ¼ yard white felt or fleece
- 16" x 30" needled cotton batting
- All-purpose thread to match fabrics
- 2 yards 18"-wide fusible web
- 6" (¼"-wide) red ribbon
- Large yo-yo maker (optional)
- Permanent fabric adhesive
- Temporary spray adhesive
- Basic sewing tools and supplies

Cutting
1. Enlarge Santa pattern 400 percent; cut one each of entire shape from white tonal, red/white print and batting.

2. Trace all shapes onto the paper side of the fusible web as directed on pieces for number to cut; cut out shapes, leaving a margin around each one.

3. Fuse shapes to the wrong side of fabrics as directed on each piece; cut out shapes on traced lines. Remove paper backing.

Making the Yo-Yos
1. Prepare 13 medium yo-yos with white/silver print and 14 medium yo-yos with white tonal using the large yo-yo maker referring to the manufacturer's instructions.

2. To prepare yo-yos without the yo-yo maker, cut (13) 4"-diameter circles white/silver print and (14) 4"-diameter circles white tonal; complete finished-edge yo-yos referring to Making Yo-Yos on page 1.

Completing the Santa Top

1. Spray the wrong side of the white tonal Santa base with temporary spray adhesive and adhere it to the batting shape with edges even; baste the layers together ⅛" from the edge.

2. Arrange and fuse the face and then the hat piece to the white Santa base referring to pattern for positioning.

3. Arrange and fuse in order on hat and face—hatband, eyebrows, eyes, mouth, mustache, nose and lips—referring to pattern for positioning.

4. Edgestitch each piece in place through all layers with thread to match fabrics.

5. Place the appliquéd face/hat/batting piece right sides together with the red/print backing; stitch all around, leaving a 6" opening on one side.

6. Turn right side out through opening; press edges flat. Turn opening edges to the inside; hand-stitch in place.

7. Make a loop with the ribbon; tack ends to the wrong side of the hat tip by hand or machine. *Note: Be sure it is secure as it is used to hang the Santa project.*

8. Hand-stitch one white/silver yo-yo to the right side of the top of the hat.

9. Arrange the remaining yo-yos on the beard area and tack in place using permanent fabric adhesive. Hand-tack the yo-yos in place or glue securely in place using more permanent fabric adhesive to finish. ❖

Yo-Yo Ho-Ho Santa
Placement Diagram 14" x 28"

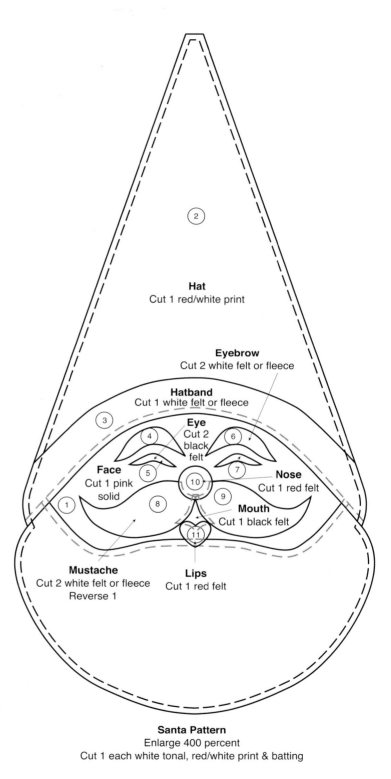

Hat
Cut 1 red/white print

Eyebrow
Cut 2 white felt or fleece

Hatband
Cut 1 white felt or fleece

Eye
Cut 2 black felt

Face
Cut 1 pink solid

Nose
Cut 1 red felt

Mouth
Cut 1 black felt

Mustache
Cut 2 white felt or fleece
Reverse 1

Lips
Cut 1 red felt

Santa Pattern
Enlarge 400 percent
Cut 1 each white tonal, red/white print & batting

Yo-Yo Snowman Place Mat, Napkin & Napkin Ring

Designs by Chris Malone

Make a simple table set using yo-yo snowmen.

Project Specifications
Skill Level: Beginner
Place Mat Size: 16" x 13"
Napkin Size: 13" x 13"
Napkin Ring Size: Approximately 2" x 2"

Materials
- Scrap orange felt
- ¼ yard or fat quarter white dot tonal
- ½ yard blue print
- ½ yard red-and-white plaid
- Batting 16½" x 13½"
- All-purpose thread to match fabrics
- 4 (¼") black shank buttons
- 3 (¾") black shank buttons
- 7 (½") white buttons
- ¾ yard ⅝"-wide red wire-edge ribbon
- White and brown size 5 pearl cotton
- Orange 6-strand embroidery floss
- Permanent fabric adhesive
- Marking pencil or air-soluble marking pen
- Large-eye embroidery needle
- Basic sewing tools and supplies

Cutting
1. Cut one 15" x 12" A rectangle blue print.

2. Cut one 16½" x 13½" backing rectangle blue print.

3. Cut one 13½" x 13½" square blue print for napkin.

4. Cut two 1¼" x 12" B strips and two 1¼" x 16½" C strips red-and-white plaid.

5. Cut two 2" x 6½" strips red-and-white plaid for snowman scarfs.

6. Cut one 13½" x 13½" square red-and-white plaid for napkin.

7. Cut one white dot tonal circle in each of the following diameters: 7½", 5½", 4" and 4¼".

8. Prepare template for nose piece; cut as directed.

Making the Yo-Yos
1. Make finished-edge yo-yos from each of the white dot tonal circles referring to Making Yo-Yos on page 1.

Yo-Yo Snowman Place Mat
Completing the Place Mat
1. Using the marking pencil, draw a gentle curving line across the right side of the A rectangle about 4" up from the bottom edge as shown in Figure 1.

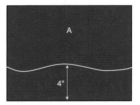

Figure 1

2. Stem-stitch along the marked line using white pearl cotton.

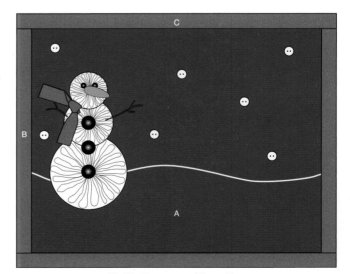

Yo-Yo Snowman Place Mat
Placement Diagram 16" x 13"

3. Arrange the largest yo-yo 2¼" up from the bottom edge and 1¼" in from the side edge of A as shown in Figure 2; place the next largest yo-yo above the larger one, overlapping ½", again referring to Figure 2. Place the smallest yo-yo on top, overlapping ¼", again referring to Figure 2.

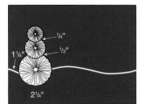

Figure 2

4. Hand-stitch the yo-yos in place all around.

5. Mark the snowman arms on each side of the center yo-yo using pattern given; embroider with a stem stitch using brown pearl cotton.

6. Sew two ¼" black buttons to the top yo-yo for eyes. Sew a ¾" black button over the center and lower yo-yo holes and the third midway between the other two.

7. Sew a B strip to the short ends and C strips to the long sides of A; press seams toward B and C strips.

8. Place the backing rectangle right side up on the batting, matching edges. Place the A-B-C rectangle right sides together with the backing; pin to hold. Sew all around, leaving a 5" opening along the bottom edge.

9. Trim batting close to seam; trim corners. Turn right side out; press edges flat. Fold in the seam allowance at the opening to the inside; hand-stitch the opening closed.

10. Topstitch in the ditch of border seams all around.

11. Arrange the seven white buttons in the area above the white line to simulate snowflakes; sew in place, stitching through all layers.

12. Fold a 2" x 6½" scarf strip in half with right sides together along length; stitch along the raw edges leaving a small opening at the center of the long edge. Trim the corners and turn right side out through opening.

13. Press edges flat. Turn seam allowance at opening to the inside and hand-stitch closed.

14. Tie a knot in the center of the scarf; tack the knot to the left side of the snowman's head.

15. Layer two nose pieces and sew a blanket stitch around the edges with 2 strands orange floss. Apply fabric adhesive to the back side of the nose at the wide end only; place over the hole in the snowman's face as shown in Figure 3 to finish.

Figure 3

Yo-Yo Snowman Napkin

Completing the Napkin

1. To make napkin, pin two 13½" x 13½" squares right sides together; sew all around, leaving a 4" opening along one edge. Trim corners; turn right side out. Press edges flat and opening seams to the inside; hand-stitch opening closed.

2. Topstitch ¼" from edge all around to finish.

Yo-Yo Snowman Napkin Ring

Completing the Napkin Ring

1. Add eyes and nose to the remaining yo-yo for snowman face referring to steps 6 and 15 in Completing the Place Mat.

2. Complete a scarf referring to steps 12–14 in Completing the Place Mat.

3. Tack or glue the back of the snowman's head to the ribbon 12" from one end as shown in Figure 4.

12"

Figure 4

4. Fold the napkin as desired and wrap the long end of the ribbon around the napkin and tie the ends in a bow at the side to use. ❖

Yo-Yo Snowman Napkin & Napkin Ring
Placement Diagram Napkin 13" x 13"
Napkin Ring 2" x 2"

Snowman Arms

Stem Stitch

Nose
Cut 4 orange felt

Blanket Stitch

Yo-Yo Puppy

Design by Carol Zentgraf

Start with a purchased stuffed-animal pattern and substitute colorful yo-yos for the legs.

Project Specifications
Skill Level: Beginner
Puppy Size: Approximately 10" tall seated

Materials
- 8 coordinating fat quarters
- All-purpose thread to match fabrics
- Purchased pattern for 10"-tall stuffed puppy or other animal
- Safety eyes and nose as indicated on pattern
- Large yo-yo maker (optional)
- Polyester fiberfill
- Waxed button thread
- 6"-long sharp decorator needle
- Permanent fabric adhesive
- Basic sewing tools and supplies

Cutting
1. Follow pattern guide sheet to cut out animal pieces from one fat quarter, eliminating all four legs.

2. For upper collar, cut a 3" x 21" strip from one fat quarter. For lower collar, cut a 4" x 21" strip from a contrasting fat quarter.

Making the Yo-Yos
1. Complete 44 assorted yo-yos using yo-yo maker and referring to manufacturer's instructions.

2. To prepare yo-yos without yo-yo maker, cut (44) 4"-diameter circles from fat quarters; complete finished-edge yo-yos referring to Making Yo-Yos on page 1.

Completing the Puppy
1. Follow pattern instructions to make and stuff head and body; attach eyes, nose and ears.
Note: Use a ¼" seam allowance throughout unless otherwise indicated; press as you sew.

2. Mark placement of legs on body.

3. Fold each collar strip in half along length with right sides together; stitch along long raw edges.

4. Turn right sides out and press flat. Turn ends in ¼"; slipstitch the two ends of each strip together to make circles.

5. Sew a gathering stitch close to the seamed edge of each strip and pull threads to slightly gather strips.

6. Place collars around puppy's neck and pull threads to gather each ruffle securely; knot thread ends.

7. Tack collar edges to neck with a small amount of fabric adhesive.

8. For forelegs, cut a long length of waxed button thread and thread one end through the eye of the decorator needle; stitching through the openings of the yo-yos, thread 10 yo-yos onto the needle, alternating colors.

9. Pull yo-yos ⅛" from the first stitching.

10. Stitch through the body at one foreleg location; mark and tie the thread ends together, pulling string of yo-yos close to the body.

11. Apply fabric adhesive to the knot to secure and lightly glue center of first yo-yo to body.

12. Repeat steps 8–11 to complete a second foreleg.

13. Make two hind legs as in steps 8–11 using 12 yo-yos for each. ❖

Yo-Yo Puppy
Placement Diagram
Approximately 10" tall seated

Yo-Yo Tic-Tac-Toe Game

Design by Mary Ayres

With a few scraps and minimal sewing time, you can make a very entertaining and portable game for use at home or during travel.

Project Specifications
Skill Level: Beginner
Board Size: Approximately 9" x 9"

Materials
- 9½" x 9½" solid or textured fabric square for top of game board
- 2 (9½" x 5¾") rectangles for backing
- 5 (4"-diameter) circles each of 2 different fabrics for playing pieces
- Muslin lining 9½" x 9½"
- Thin batting 9½" x 9½"
- All-purpose thread to match fabrics and black
- 2½ yards black jumbo rickrack
- Water-soluble marker
- Basic sewing tools and supplies

Making the Yo-Yos
1. Complete five finished-edge yo-yos each of two different fabrics referring to Making Yo-Yos on page 1. Flatten yo-yos to make playing pieces.

Yo-Yo Tic-Tac-Toe Game
Placement Diagram Approximately 9" x 9"

Completing the Game Board
1. Mark a line 3¼" in from each edge on the right side of the 9½" x 9½" fabric square using a water-soluble marker referring to Figure 1.

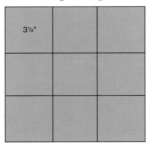

Figure 1

2. Sandwich the batting square between the wrong side of the marked square and the lining square; pin or baste to hold layers flat.

3. Cut eight 9½" pieces black jumbo rickrack; sew a piece on each marked line, and on each outside edge, matching edge of rickrack with edge and stitching through the center of rickrack.

4. Turn one long edge of each backing rectangle under ¼"; press. Turn under ¼"; press and stitch to hem.

5. Pin backing pieces right sides together with the stitched top with hemmed edges of backing overlapping as shown in Figure 2; stitch all around.

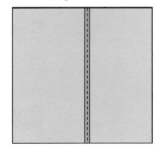

Figure 2

6. Store the yo-yo playing pieces inside the game board when not in use. ❖

Yo-Yo Star Flowers

Design by Marian Shenk

Angled seams on a striped border print come together for an intriguing frame on this candle mat.

Project Specifications
Skill Level: Beginner
Candle Mat Size: Approximately 16" x 16"

Materials
- 14" x 14" square white tonal
- Scraps of blue and green for appliqué
- 4 gold print 2"-diameter circles for yo-yos
- ¼ yard border fabric with 2" stripe
- ¼ yard navy tonal
- Backing 18" x 18"
- Thin batting 18" x 18"
- ¼ yard fusible web
- ¼ yard fabric stabilizer
- 4 (½") blue buttons
- 1 yard brown quick-bias
- Machine-embroidery thread to match appliqué fabrics
- All-purpose thread to blend with fabrics
- White quilting thread
- Basic sewing tools and supplies

Cutting
1. Prepare templates using pattern pieces given; cut border pieces as directed on pattern.

2. Fold 14" x 14" white tonal square in eighths; place background template on folds and cut bottom edge.

3. Cut two 2¼" by fabric width strips navy tonal for binding.

4. Trace appliqué shapes onto the paper side of the fusible web referring to patterns for number to trace; cut out shapes, leaving a margin around each one.

5. Fuse shapes to fabrics as directed on patterns; cut out on traced lines. Remove paper backing.

Making the Yo-Yos
1. Make finished-edge yo-yos from 2" gold print circles referring to Making Yo-Yos on page 1.

Completing the Candle Mat
1. Draw a 7½" circle in the center of the background

octagon. Cover this line with brown quick-bias; fuse. Hand-appliqué with matching thread to secure.

2. Referring to Placement Diagram, arrange appliqué shapes on background; fuse.

3. Machine-appliqué around fused shapes with matching machine-embroidery threads using a close machine satin stitch.

4. Fasten yo-yos to the center of each star flower with one blue button.

5. Sew border pieces together on short ends to make octagon, carefully matching the stripes.

6. Hand-appliqué border to outer edge of white octagon; press.

7. Mark one star-flower shape in center for quilting.

8. Sandwich batting between completed top and prepared backing; pin or baste to hold.

9. Hand-quilt around outside edges of appliqué shapes, on marked lines and in the ditch around border.

10. When quilting is complete, trim edges even; remove pins or basting.

11. Join binding strips on short ends with diagonal seams to make one long strip; trim seams to ¼" and press seams open. Fold the strip in half along length with wrong sides together; press.

12. Sew binding to the right side of the candle mat edges, overlapping ends. Fold binding to the back side and stitch in place. ❖

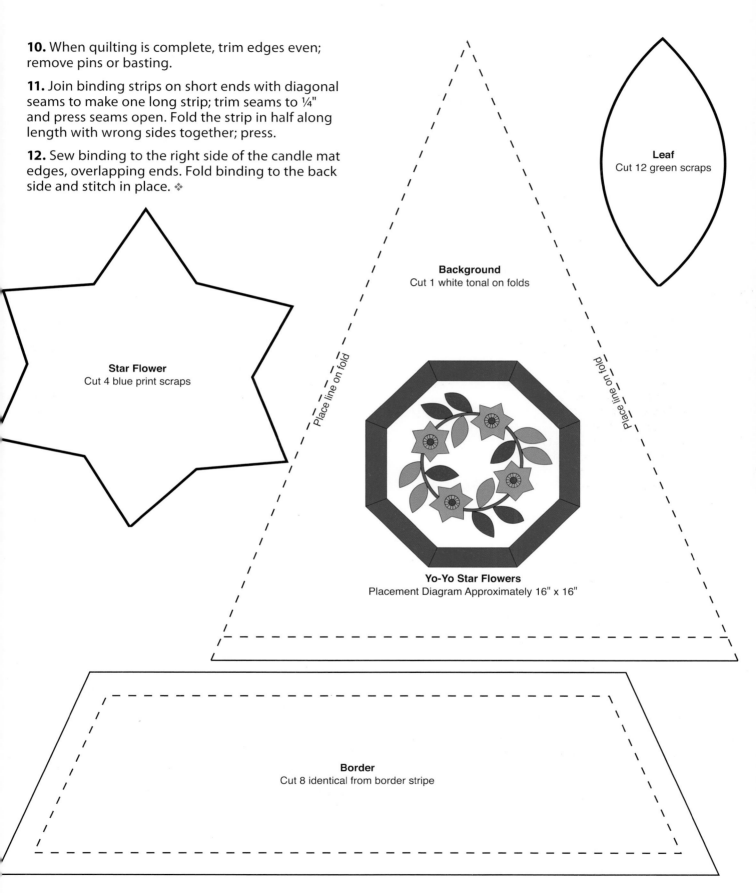

Leaf
Cut 12 green scraps

Background
Cut 1 white tonal on folds

Place line on fold

Place line on fold

Star Flower
Cut 4 blue print scraps

Yo-Yo Star Flowers
Placement Diagram Approximately 16" x 16"

Border
Cut 8 identical from border stripe

Yo-Yo Star Table Topper

Design by Chris Malone

Star shapes are appliquéd to a background made of yo-yos to make an unusual table topper.

Project Specifications
Skill Level: Beginner
Topper Size: 20" x 16"

Materials
- Assorted red, green, blue and tan scraps
- ⅜ yard gold mottled
- ¾ yard quilter's fleece
- All-purpose thread to match fabrics
- 5 (⅞") shank buttons
- Permanent fabric adhesive
- Basic sewing tools and supplies

Cutting
1. Cut (80) 4½"-diameter circles assorted scraps for yo-yos.

2. Cut five 2"-diameter circles from one scrap for buttons.

3. Cut (80) 2"-diameter circles from quilter's fleece.

4. Cut a 1" x 1" square of fabric to match each yo-yo fabric circle.

Making the Yo-Yos
1. Center a fleece circle on the wrong side of a fabric circle; secure in place with a dot of permanent fabric adhesive.

2. Center a 1" x 1" square to match the fabric circle on the fleece; secure in place with a dot of permanent fabric adhesive. *Note: This scrap covers the quilter's fleece so it does not show in the center of the finished yo-yo.*

3. Complete 80 finished-edge yo-yos referring to Making Yo-Yos on page 1, using layered circles.

Completing the Table Topper
1. Arrange yo-yos in eight rows of 10 yo-yos each.

2. To join, hold two yo-yos together with gathered sides facing; take 3 or 4 small stitches right at the edge of the circle as shown in Figure 1. Unfold the pair and add a third yo-yo in the same manner; repeat with 10 yo-yos to complete a row. Repeat to make eight rows; join rows in the same manner to complete the yo-yo base.

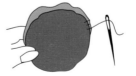

Figure 1

3. Prepare templates for star shapes using patterns given.

4. To make star appliqués, fold the gold mottled fabric in half with right sides together; trace three large and two small stars on one side.

5. Layer the traced fabric with the quilter's fleece; pin. Sew all around on traced lines through all layers; cut out ⅛" from stitched seams.

Clip into corners and trim points; trim fleece very close to stitching.

6. Cut a slash through the top layer of fabric only; turn star shapes right side out through opening. Press. Slipstitch the opening closed. Topstitch ¼" from outer edge of star all around with matching thread.

7. To cover each button, fold edge of button circle and hand-sew as for yo-yo. Place a shank button in the center of the fabric and pull stitches tightly around the shank. Knot thread; sew button to the center of a star.

8. Referring to the Placement Diagram and photo of topper, arrange the stars on the yo-yo base; apply dots of permanent fabric adhesive to the back of the star shapes where they touch a yo-yo to complete the topper. ❖

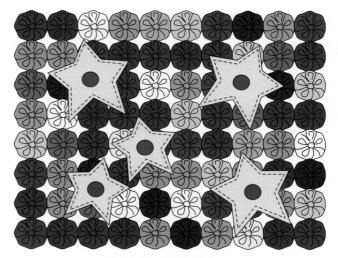

Yo-Yo Star Table Topper
Placement Diagram 20" x 16"

Large Star

Small Star

Yo-Yo Basket

Design by Janice McKee

Gathered fabric circles are joined to make a distinctive home decor accent.

Project Note

The sample was made using a bowl with a 10¼" diameter at the top and 6½" diameter at the bottom for the mold. Depending on the bowl used, fewer or more yo-yos may be needed.

Project Specifications

Skill Level: Beginner
Basket Size: Size varies

Materials

- ½ yard each red, white and navy blue prints
- All-purpose thread to match fabrics
- Fabric stiffener
- Plastic wrap
- Bowl to use as a mold
- Basic sewing tools and supplies

Cutting

1. Cut (22) 3¼"-diameter circles from each fabric to total 66.

2. Cut one each red and blue print 7½"-diameter circles.

Making the Yo-Yos

1. Complete finished-edge yo-yos using small circles referring to Making Yo-Yos on page 1.

Completing the Basket

1. Stitch small yo-yos together in rows, one row of each color. Sew rows together, staggering the center row between the top and bottom rows.

2. Sew constructed piece together at side to cover sides of bowl (try on for fit), easing and sewing tighter as necessary.

3. Turn under edges of 7½"-diameter circles ¼"; press. Layer the circles with wrong sides together; slipstitch edges together.

4. Turn bowl mold upside down on work surface; center the large circles (bottom of basket) on bowl bottom. Slip yo-yos (basket sides) over the bowl. Pin bottom and sides together; remove from bowl. Stitch, easing in where necessary.

5. Cover bowl mold with plastic wrap.

6. Place stitched fabric over the plastic and saturate with fabric stiffener, molding yo-yo shape to bowl, referring to manufacturer's instructions. Let dry. Remove bowl and plastic wrap. ❖

Yo-Yo Basket
Placement Diagram Size Varies

Sleepy-Time Yo-Yo Bedding

Design by Patsy Moreland

Bedtime is a time of relaxation, and what better way to relax than in these pretty yo-yo-embellished sheets. Yo-yos are a great way to use up scrap fabric to enhance wearables and home decor.

Project Specifications
Skill Level: Beginner
Yo-yos fit 2 pillowcases and 1 flat sheet

Materials
- ¼ yard each variety of prints
- 2 pillowcases
- 1 flat bed sheet
- All-purpose thread to match fabrics
- Air-soluble marking pen (optional)
- Basic sewing tools and supplies

Cutting
Note: *Wash, dry and steam-press fabrics, sheet and pillowcases.*

1. Cutting through three layers of fabric at a time, cut a total of (18) 3¼" A circles and (41) 2½" B circles from prints.

Making the Yo-Yos
1. Make finished-edge yo-yos from the cut circles referring to Making Yo-Yos on page 1.

Completing the Yo-Yo Appliqué
1. Using an air-soluble marker or basting stitches, mark the center length and width of borders on pillowcases and sheet referring to Figure 1.

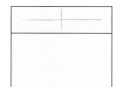

Figure 1

2. Pin one large (A) yo-yo next to center of border. Referring to Figure 2, add additional yo-yos. Continue in this pattern to pin yo-yos across borders of pillowcases and sheet.

3. Hand-stitch yo-yos in place around edges using all-purpose thread and small stitches. ❖

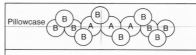

Figure 2

House of White Birches, Berne, Indiana 46711   Clotilde.com

Flannel Yo-Yo Throw

Design by Chris Malone

Flannel makes the perfect throw or lap quilt to keep warm on cold winter days.

Project Specifications
Skill Level: Beginner
Quilt Size: 41" x 41"

Materials
- 8 fat quarters coordinating flannel prints, solids or tonals
- 1⅓ yards cream print flannel
- Batting 47" x 47"
- Backing 47" x 47"
- All-purpose thread to match fabrics
- Quilting thread
- Size 5 pearl cotton to coordinate with flannels
- Large-eye embroidery needle
- Permanent fabric adhesive
- Basic sewing tools and supplies

Cutting
1. Prewash all flannel fabrics.

2. Cut 39 total 5½" x 5½" A squares total coordinating flannel prints, solids or tonals.

3. Cut 21 total 6½"-diameter circles coordinating flannel prints, solids or tonals.

4. Cut three 6½"-diameter circles cream print flannel.

5. Cut two 5½" by fabric width strips cream print flannel; subcut strips into (10) 5½" A squares cream print flannel.

6. Cut two 3½" x 35½" B strips and two 3½" x 41½" C strips cream print flannel.

7. Cut five 2½" by fabric width strips cream print for binding.

Making the Yo-Yos
1. If the wrong side of the flannel is very light and contrasts with the right side, cut a 1½" x 1½" square of matching flannel and place it in the center of the wrong side of a matching 6½"-diameter circle.

2. Apply small dots of fabric adhesive on each corner of the squares to secure. Fold in a full ¼" around the edge of each 6½"-diameter circle. ***Note: Because the opening in a flannel yo-yo will not close as tightly as a yo-yo made from lighter-weight fabric, the open center will match the right side of the fabric with the application of this small square.***

3. Complete 24 finished-edge yo-yos referring to Making Yo-Yos on page 1.

Completing the Top
1. Arrange and join the 49 A squares in seven rows of seven squares each, varying the placement of the colors; press seams in adjoining rows in opposite directions. ***Note: If you prefer, the yo-yos may be arranged and attached before the squares are joined in rows and the pieced top is complete.***

2. Join the rows as arranged to complete the pieced center; press seams in one direction.

3. Center a contrasting yo-yo on alternating blocks referring to the Placement Diagram for positioning; pin or apply a few dots of fabric adhesive to the back side of each yo-yo to hold in place for stitching.

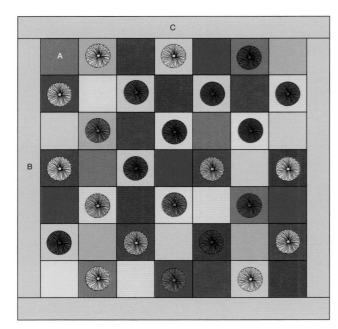

Flannel Yo-Yo Throw
Placement Diagram 41" x 41"

4. Select pearl cotton to coordinate with the first yo-yo that will be stitched in place. Cut a piece 18"–20" long; knot end. Thread through the large-eye needle.

5. Using a single strand and starting underneath the edge of the yo-yo to hide the knot, blanket-stitch all around the edge of the yo-yo to attach to the background as shown in Figure 1, securing end on the back side of the background square.

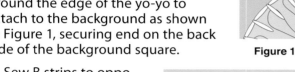

Figure 1

6. Sew B strips to opposite sides and C strips to the top and bottom of the pieced center; press seams toward B and C strips to complete the pieced top.

Completing the Quilt

1. Sandwich the batting between the completed top and prepared backing; pin or baste layers together to hold.

2. Quilt as desired by hand or machine; remove pins or basting. Trim excess backing and batting even with quilt top.

3. Join binding strips on short ends with diagonal seams to make one long strip; trim seams to ¼" and press seams open. Fold the strip in half along length with wrong sides together; press.

4. Sew binding to the right side of the quilt edges, overlapping ends. Fold binding to the back side and stitch in place.

5. Thread the embroidery needle with 2 strands of pearl cotton to match the color used to attach yo-yo. Separate into

4 strands. From the top, take a small stitch in the center of each yo-yo through all layers. Bring the needle back out on the top, leaving a 3" tail as shown in Figure 2. Tie the strands into a double knot and trim ends to 1", again referring to Figure 2, to complete the quilt. ❖

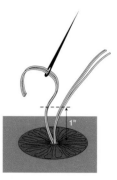

Figure 2

Peekaboo Yo-Yo Quilt

Design by Betty Alderman

Twinkling stars and peekaboo yo-yos make this quilt a sparkling addition to any collection.

Project Specifications
Skill Level: Beginner
Quilt Size: 25½" x 30½"
Block Size: 4" x 4"
Number of Blocks: 20

Materials
- ⅛ yard each of 20 different navy, tan and red prints
- ⅔ yard navy star print
- 1⅜ yards cream solid
- Backing 32" x 37"
- Batting 32" x 37"
- All-purpose thread to match fabrics
- 2 skeins navy 6-strand embroidery floss
- ⅛ yard 18"-wide fusible web
- Basic sewing tools and supplies

Peekaboo Yo-Yo Quilt
Placement Diagram 25½" x 30½"

Cutting

1. For one Star block, cut eight 1½" x 1½" C squares and one 2½" x 2½" A square from the same navy, tan or red print. Repeat cutting for 20 Star blocks.

2. Cut (50) 3½"-diameter circles cream solid for yo-yos.

3. Trace 20 peekaboo circles onto the paper side of the fusible web; cut out circles, leaving a margin around each one. Fuse a circle to the wrong side of each navy, tan and red print; cut out on traced lines. Remove paper backing.

4. Cut eight 1½" by fabric width strips cream solid; subcut strips into (80) 2½" B rectangles and (80) 1½" D squares.

5. Cut one 4½" by fabric width strip cream solid; subcut strip into (16) 1½" E strips.

6. Cut five 1½" x 24½" F strips cream solid.

7. Cut two strips 1½" x 21½" G strips cream solid.

8. Cut two 2¾" x 21½" H strips and two 2¾" x 31" I strips navy star print.

9. Cut three 2¼" by fabric strips navy star print for binding.

Making the Yo-Yos

1. Fold and crease each yo-yo circle to mark the center.

2. Fuse a peekaboo circle on the center of the wrong side of 20 yo-yo circles as shown in Figure 1 to create the peekaboo area.

3. Make 20 finished-edge yo-yos with peekaboo centers and 30 folded-edge plain yo-yos referring to Making Yo-Yos on page 1.

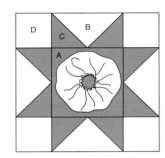

Star
4" x 4" Block
Make 20

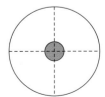

Figure 1

Completing the Star Blocks

1. Draw a diagonal line from corner to corner on the wrong side of each C square.

2. To complete one Star block, select same-fabric A and C squares.

3. Place a C square on one end of B and stitch on the marked line as shown in Figure 2; trim seam to ¼" and press C to the right side.

Figure 2   **Figure 3**

4. Repeat step 3 on the remaining end of B to complete one B-C unit referring to Figure 3.

5. Repeat steps 3 and 4 to complete eight matching B-C units.

6. Sew a B-C unit to opposite sides of A to make an A-B-C unit as shown in Figure 4; press seams toward A.

Figure 4   **Figure 5**

7. Sew D to opposite ends of the remaining two B-C units to complete a B-C-D row as shown in Figure 5; press seams toward D. Repeat to make two B-C-D rows.

8. Sew a B-C-D row to opposite sides of the A-B-C unit to complete one Star block referring to the block drawing; press seams toward the A-B-C unit.

9. Blindstitch a yo-yo with a matching fabric peekaboo circle in the center of A using thread to match yo-yo to complete the Star block.

10. Repeat steps 2–9 to complete 20 Star blocks.

Completing the Top

1. Join five Star blocks with four E strips to make a vertical row as shown in Figure 6; press seams toward E strips. Repeat to make four vertical rows.

2. Join the vertical rows with five F strips; press seams toward F strips.

3. Sew a G strip to the top and bottom of the pieced center; press seams toward G strips.

E

Figure 6

4. Sew H strips to the top and bottom, and I strips to opposite long sides of the pieced center; press seams toward H and I strips to complete the pieced top.

5. Appliqué a plain yo-yo at each E-F intersection, referring to the Placement Diagram for positioning.

Completing the Quilt

1. Sandwich the batting between the completed top and prepared backing; pin or baste layers together to hold.

2. Using 6 strands of navy embroidery floss, make a tie through all layers, in the center of each plain yo-yo at sashing intersections. Make more ties in the border to secure all layers. ***Note:*** *If you prefer, quilt the layers together.*

3. When tying is complete, remove pins or basting. Trim excess backing and batting even with quilt top.

4. Join binding strips on short ends with diagonal seams to make one long strip; trim seams to ¼" and press seams open. Fold the strip in half along length with wrong sides together; press.

5. Sew binding to the right side of the quilt edges, overlapping ends. Fold binding to the back side and stitch in place to finish. ❖

Peekaboo Circle
Trace 20 on fusible web

Blooming Yo-Yo Garden

Design by Marian Shenk

Buttons and yo-yos bloom in profusion on this colorful little garden wall quilt.

Project Specifications
Skill Level: Intermediate
Wall Quilt Size: 27" x 27"
Block Size: 9½" x 9½"
Number of Blocks: 4

Materials
- ⅛ yard green tonal
- ¼ yard each orange, pale blue, pink, yellow and purple prints
- 1 yard dark blue print
- Backing 33" x 33"
- Batting 33" x 33"
- All-purpose thread to match fabrics
- Natural-color quilting thread
- 16 (½") buttons to match yo-yos
- Basic sewing tools and supplies

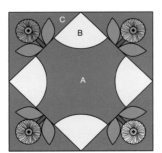

Blooming Yo-Yo
9½" x 9½" Block
Make 4

Cutting
1. Prepare templates for pieces A and B; cut as directed on each piece.

2. Cut a ½" x 20" strip green tonal; fold under ⅛" on each long edge and press. Cut strip into (16) 1¼" segments for stems.

3. Cut four 3¾"-diameter yo-yo circles from yellow, pink, purple and orange prints.

4. Prepare template for leaf using pattern given; cut as directed on piece, adding ⅛"–¼" seam allowance all around when cutting.

5. Cut two 1½" by fabric width strips each pink, yellow, purple and dark blue prints; subcut strips into four each 19½" D strips.

6. Cut two 5⅝" by fabric width strips dark blue print; subcut strips into eight 5⅝" squares. Cut each square in half on one diagonal to make 16 C triangles. Fold each triangle in half along long diagonal edge and crease to mark the center.

7. Cut the remainder of the 5⅝" strip from step 6 into four 4½" x 4½" E squares dark blue print.

8. Cut three 2¼" by fabric width strips dark blue print for binding.

Making the Yo-Yo Flowers
1. Referring to Making Yo-Yos on page 1, make 16 finished-edge yo-yos for flowers using orange, pink, yellow and purple prints.

2. Sew a button to the center of each yo-yo.

Completing the Blooming Yo-Yo Blocks
1. Place a stem piece on the creased line perpendicular to long edge on each C as shown in Figure 1; hand-appliqué in place.

Figure 1

2. To complete one block, fold and crease curved edges of A and B pieces to mark the centers.

3. Matching creased lines, sew B to each curved edge of A to complete an A-B unit as shown in Figure 2; press seams toward A.

Figure 2

4. Sew a C triangle to each side of the A-B unit; press seams toward C.

5. Turn under seam allowance on each leaf shape; place a leaf on each side of each stem piece. Hand-appliqué in place.

6. Hand-stitch a yo-yo flower at the tip of each stem to complete one block.

7. Repeat steps 2–6 to complete four Blooming Yo-Yo blocks.

Completing the Top
1. Join two Blooming Yo-Yo blocks to make a row; press seams in one direction. Repeat to make two rows.

2. Join the rows to complete the pieced center; press seam in one direction.

3. Join one each color D strip along length to make a D border strip referring to the Placement Diagram for color order; press seams in one direction. Repeat to make four pieced D strips.

4. Sew a pieced D strip to opposite sides of the pieced center; press seams toward D strips.

5. Sew an E square to each end of each remaining pieced D strip; press seams away from E.

6. Sew an E/D strip to the remaining sides of the pieced center to complete the pieced top.

Completing the Quilt
1. Sandwich the batting between the completed top and prepared backing; pin or baste layers together to hold.

2. Quilt as desired by hand or machine; remove pins or basting. Trim excess backing and batting even with quilt top.

3. Join binding strips on short ends with diagonal seams to make one long strip; trim seams to ¼" and press seams open. Fold the strip in half along length with wrong sides together; press.

4. Sew binding to the right side of the quilt edges, overlapping ends. Fold binding to the back side and stitch in place to finish. ❖

House of White Birches, Berne, Indiana 46711   Clotilde.com

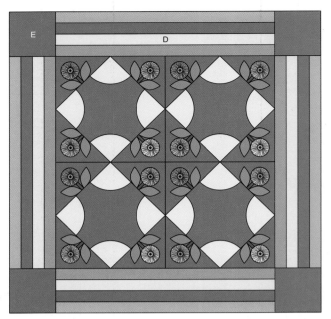

Blooming Yo-Yo Garden
Placement Diagram 27" x 27"

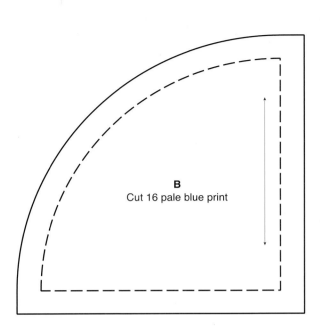

B
Cut 16 pale blue print

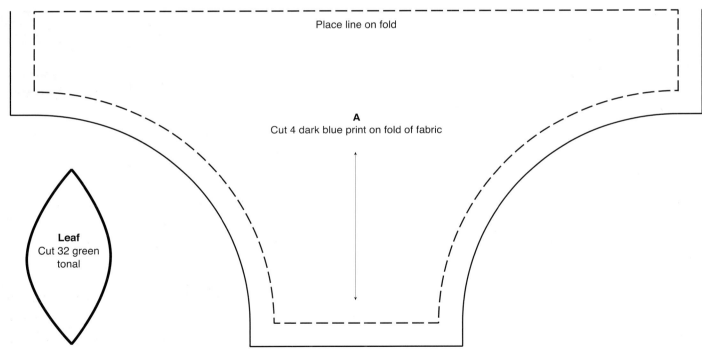

Place line on fold

A
Cut 4 dark blue print on fold of fabric

Leaf
Cut 32 green
tonal

HOUSE of WHITE BIRCHES
PUBLISHERS SINCE 1947

Yo-Yo Quilting is published by DRG, 306 East Parr Road, Berne, IN 46711. Printed in USA. Copyright © 2010 DRG. All rights reserved.
This publication may not be reproduced in part or in whole without written permission from the publisher.

RETAIL STORES: If you would like to carry this pattern book or any other DRG publications, visit DRGwholesale.com

Every effort has been made to ensure that the instructions in this pattern book are complete and accurate. We cannot, however, take responsibility
for human error, typographical mistakes or variations in individual work. Please visit ClotildeCustomerCare.com to check for pattern updates.

ISBN: 978-1-59217-291-7
5 6 7 8 9